Wet Moments

poems by

Len Chernila

Florecer

First Edition

Published by
Florecer
Denver, Colorado
florecerpublishing@gmail.com

Copyright © 2010 by Len Chernila

All rights reserved. No part of this book may be used or reproduced by any means whatsoever, either electronic or mechanical, without written permission from the author, except in the case of brief quotations embodied in critical articles and reviews.

The Wet Moment / by Len Chernila – 1st ed.

Edited by Dianna Shivvers

ISBN 978-0-6155-2173-2

FIRST SOFTCOVER PRINTING, 2011
Printed in The United States of America

Dedicated to LizAnn Lynch

Acknowledging the poetry of
Tony Scibella and Don Becker.

Thank you for inspiring me and
helping me with my work

Table of Contents

Introduction	vii
The Wet Moment	1
I write for the Lady	2
The Stuff of Dreams	3
The Truth Is. . .	4
Humble before Creation,	
Proud in one another's Arms	5
Danger	6
Visionary Company of Love	7
The Loving Deed	8
Justice	9
Bring Me Along	10
What the Fuck Part Two	11
Ride Hard	12
Listening	13
I am a Star	14
The Conspiracy of Silence	15
Am I right? Am I right?	16
Soul Sex	17
Yeah, You!	18
Vanity Isn't Much To Warm To	19
What Do Women Want	20
Stop – Be Chill	21
Looking At The World	22
More Lovely Than Ever	23
Time After Time You Get It Right	24
untitled	25
Destination Home	26
I want, I want	27
Aphorisms	28
I love your fighting style	29
3 Score and Ten	30
Carry That Weight	31
Eyes on the Prize, Freedom	32
There's Something I Can Do	33
Time Flowers	34
Your Storm	36
My Time has Come and it's Apocalypse!	37
The Lesbian Challenge	38
Long Story Short	39
Go Home to Mama	40
Drop Me Like a Cat	41
Shut This Shit Down	42

Introduction

Wet Moments come frequently, yet sometimes we cannot see or feel them because of distractions, disbelief or the struggles of daily life. Wet Moments are the possibility for change, for adventure, for creativity, for spectacular things to happen. Open up to your own Wet Moments; you may be surprised by what you discover.

Awareness is the first step. Len Chernila's poems challenge the reader, the listener, to not only be aware but to take action, to grab hold of what is precious and fleeting. The power and magic of Len's poetry, and especially his spoken word art, lie in open-ended challenges that inspire others to embrace and to work with their own Wet Moments.

Len Chernila's poetry exemplifies the Wet Moment through action and expression. If you've ever had the pleasure of listening to Len on the mic at poetry events or joining him in conversation, you'll know what I mean. Oftentimes, mid-performance, Len is known to say, "I did not know I was going to say that. You think I know what I'm doing?" While his delivery of this statement seems quite humorous, it reflects how much his performances, his poems, truly are *in the moment*, playing with what is rich and ripe and fresh and new. He crafts poems reflective of possibility, open for personal interpretation, filled with the momentary freshness of inspiration opening the door for anything to happen. Wide-open, Len's poems "possibilize" life, staying clear of specific definitions or judgments, allowing each person to find his or her own meaning at whatever time is relevant to them. They are "Time Flowers" that go off, explode and blossom – maybe today, maybe many years later. Either way, the meaning they hold is personal to everyone who hears or reads them – interpretation and insights into humanity are available to each person. Possibility.

Len's poetry embraces many themes: love and friendship, choice and freedom, strength and perseverance, involvement, compassion and connection. His broad range and inspiring tone encourage people to sharpen their desire to achieve their own purpose. His willingness to dig to the core, the place where people cling to the dark that keeps them bound, challenges readers and listeners to stand up against limiting beliefs, to fight their own fight, to break free and soar.

~Dianna Shivvers

*The Wet Moment:
The brief interlude before
an experience dries on memory
and is referenced for future use;
the moment when
anything is possible.*

~Len Chernila

Wet Moments

The Wet Moment

When you talk to me of what you know,
I am mildly interested – after all, I like you
and you like me enough to talk to me at all –
but the talk is backwards reflecting,
about what's done or already known.

When you begin to talk of what you are
as yet uncertain, I become wildly interested!
You don't know yet? Excellent!
Perhaps we'll get somewhere!

Perhaps we'll get to the wet moment,
unfolding, seedling-like,
all in a sunny morning.

Miracle of the unknown coming into view.
Miracle for you because you are most human
in becoming human.
Miracle for me because <u>there</u> life is most intense.
The wet moment.

I write for the Lady

She of the thousand eyes
and mighty heart,
She who sets souls free –
and births bright visions,
I write for her,
for the Muse, the Goddess, the Lady.

I write for the Lady now.

Every impulse is toward touching,
dancing and drumming,
and dreaming.
She for whom I play:
my Lady.

I write poems
for the Lady.
I don't know what to do with my dream
but she <u>does</u>!
Lady does!

O Lady,
meet me at the crossroads of your dreams.
I'm coming,
O Lady,
you be there, hear?

The Stuff of Dreams

I haven't taken on.
I am equal to the load.
My Energy is my Way.
From the ground
from the underground,
from the underground springs,
I give and receive
the stuff of dreams,
I seek the fruition of vision:
fulfillment.
I find it, singing all along the way:
nothing can stop the power of a good idea
whose time has come.

The Truth Is. . .

The Encounter <u>is</u> the Truth.
It's not <u>out</u> there,
facts and their arrangements are the ground,
not the view.
The Truth is in the meeting with the unknown,
the dangerous, the tempting,
the thrill of the chase and capture,
the peace that follows. With
Real Truth – what you bring to the Encounter,
the outcome is uncertain
your actions help determine it.

The Truth is in the unplanned initiatives
which you bring to the critical meeting.
You don't know what Truth you're making –
only that what you bring tips the scales in your favor.
High stakes and your best game.
Put your energy into the Encounter with the unknown.

Humble before Creation,
Proud in one another's Arms

Yes, yes, you love him because of how
he makes you feel –
but you also love him also because of
how <u>you</u> make <u>him</u> feel!

Yes, yes, you love her because of how
she makes you feel –
but you also love her also because of
how <u>you</u> make <u>her</u> feel!

Humble before Creation,
proud in one another's arms,
you do it, you love:
you are an action partner in Creation;
you can feel; you can stir feelings
in your lover – both of you thrill to the touch.
Humble before Creation
proud in one another's arms.

Danger

I <u>am</u> danger!
I used to live <u>with</u> danger,
but it cried,
"Take me in!"
I did and now
I am the danger
I am looking for.

Visionary Company of Love

We have fun without tryin'
and when we do try
we have <u>lots</u> of fun!

We are the visionary company of love
and we love what we do.
We lift up the fallen,
we play out among equals,
and we dream of even more
of what we already enjoy:
good music, good food, good conversation.

We not only survive,
we come alive and thrive!

We are the visionary company of love.

This is no time to be humble;
that hound won't hunt.
We are proud to be out from under the whip –
we are even prouder of the games we play
and the game players who inspire us.

We are the visionary company of love
and we love what we do.

The Loving Deed

"Don't talk to me about love, baby.
Let's just go walkin' in the rain."
~ Billie Holiday

I've got nothing against love,
I've got a grudge against <u>talking</u>!

Keep it minimal –
do the loving deed,
coupla words,
<u>more</u> feeling,
<u>much</u> more silent,
loving ways.

With words – more is less.
Don't step on your own game.
Talk when it matters,
otherwise be cool,
listen more than you talk.

Don't talk to me about love, baby.
Let's just go walkin' in the rain.

Justice

Justice without compassion is murder.

Truth without kindness is a lie.

Love without freedom is sexual slavery.

Knowledge without experience is disease,
and oh, yes, life without adventure is death.

Oh, you're just exaggerating.

Yeah, right,
and you're just siding with the enemy.

Too much caution
in speech
is arsenic in the pie.

And yeah, I'm exaggerating –

SO YOU CAN FEEL IT
as well as understand!

Bring Me Along

Don't tell me nothin'!
Don't show me a goddamn thing!
Just bring me along for the ride.
I'll pick things up
any which way.
Take me along,
I'll care for myself.
Just bring me along
for the ride!
I'll make room
without getting in the way.

Take me along.

I catch on quick.
I'll make my own way.
I'll pull my weight.
I'll ride shotgun
without being a backseat driver.

Take me along for the ride.

What the Fuck Part Two

Everyday, we weave the tapestry our life,
and every night, it unravels beneath our feet.

What the Fuck!

We put it together,
it falls apart.

WTF!

However, we dress it up,
it's still tossed salad,
and whatever we think, or do
it's still just one damn thing after another!

What the fuuuuuuuuck!

Ride Hard

If you can't take the heat,
cool off at home.

If the rush hour
has run you over,
kick back, be chill,
you've got at least
two shots every day
to get back in the game.

I won't say don't quit,
with you, it's never a question of courage.

When you find your rhythm,
you'll be up and on your game –
the wheel turns –
ride hard.

Listening

You can tell if someone's listening
by the way they answer:

If the answer is <u>another</u> subject,
<u>they're not listening!</u>

If the answer starts
before you have your say,
<u>they're not listening!</u>

And

If their answer brings you down,
makes you feel left out,
pushed aside,
<u>they're not listening!</u>

In every case
you have the right to say
<u>you're not listening!</u>

But if their answer challenges you fairly,
shows some warmth, humor,
pushes your buttons
without pissing you off,
if what they say makes you feel good
about what <u>you</u> say,
then they're <u>really</u> listening.

No one has to wimp out in conversation,
neither do they have to be an asshole.

All anybody wants is a human response,
good-humored, curious and open…

If you <u>don't</u> get what you deserve,
speak right out and say:

<u>You're not listening!!</u>

I am a Star

I am not filler,
not background noise, no.
Nor window trimming either.

I don't need it all –
just my fair share –
to play out enough so
that people can <u>feel</u>
the noise, the burn, the wonder.

I am a Star.

The Conspiracy of Silence

Men can learn to love and listen,
to respect and appreciate women.
Women can feel honestly right now,
while men, at later stages of development,
can learn to help their women
to help <u>them</u>.
No secrets,
no control
or manipulation:
Respect and kindness all the way,
from dating
to reality-loving.

Am I right? Am I right?

When the world convinces a girl
that she is <u>really</u> beautiful,
she stops putting on clothes
and begins <u>dressing up</u>!

Am I right? Am I right?

Soon dressing up becomes a coronation
and as Queenie takes herself seriously,
glitter and shine come to rule.

Am I right? Am I right?

Then, when Prince Charming comes
to take off her party dress,
she gets really scared;
she feels the prince is
<u>stripping her of her crown</u>!

Am I right? Am I right?

Soul Sex

He says
<u>he</u> knows how to do it.

KMPHNNFF!

She says
<u>she</u> knows how to do it.

KMPHNNFF!

God says
they think <u>they</u> know how to do it!

KMPHNNFF!

Yoga, Sufi, Kaballah, Tantra says

Until sexuality and spirituality
are experienced together

NO ONE KNOWS HOW TO DO IT!

But we can all learn…

Yeah, You!

Stay on the hardcore tip,
in the lying world,
aim for the real.
No way over and around,
only through it,
bite the bullet
and get to it –
nothing makes it easier,
nobody knows better than you.
Do what you have to do!
Stay on the hardcore tip,
in the cut,
in the blood of the cut.

Like a baby cutting a new tooth
through the gums,
scream a little,
bite down a lot
and get 'er done.
Yeah, there's
music and laughter,
sex and drugs,
but that's all for later.
It doesn't get easier.
Work it.
Work it now.
There's only you and the work.
Get to it.
Get 'er done.
Yeah, you!

Vanity Isn't Much To Warm To

If you're good at what you do –
cool like that
proud of your ability,
'tsall good 24/7.

But if you're <u>vain</u> about
what you do,
it's like BENGAY
on your crotch,
warm at first,
then burns like hell!

Vanity isn't much
to warm to –
over time you get burned…

Better to shake off
false pride:
the real payoff is in self-satisfaction
for a job well done.

Vanity isn't much to warm to.

What Do Women Want

Women want passion
tinged with danger, laced
with kindness,
they want lots of cuddling
and real talk
right after.

They want control
of the shape of the relationship,
not everyday
but overall.

They want neck, ear, and breast,
kisses, nothing too fast, easy.

Sex packaged as romantic love,
unwrapped as pleasure,
kindness, and appreciation.

Firm yet gentle,
sweet spot touch,
they want a man to purr,
to roar deep, not loud,
to speak the little that says so much,
not you're the most wonderful,
most beautiful, most blahbity blah
But yes! There! Mmmmm….
They want a guy who can come on
and get off <u>cool</u>,
they don't want to be made self-conscious,
they don't want talk about <u>anyone</u> else,
they don't want comparisons,
they want love.

Stop – Be Chill

When what you've got
is good enough,
Stop!

Never mind what dad said
about always keep pushin',
"Be chill," is good for now.

When mom said,
"Make sure it's all alright.
<u>Always</u> drive toward your ultimate goal."
Stop!
She was right for <u>then</u>.

That's not gonna make it to Broadway,
not gonna take the cake.
Stop!
Now, kick back and enjoy what's enough.

It's a new world –
get you a taste of paradise – here and <u>now</u>.
Never was a better time.

All mom and dad wanted was <u>your good</u> –
Well that's good enough –
your good,
what you say goes –
be chill.

Looking At The World

Looking at the world
from above is a distortion
based on gods
set way above fear.

We'd have a better view
if we walked on all fours
like the rest of the mammals.

But we <u>don't</u>;
we walk up<u>right</u>
and we have to learn
to live with our distorted view
of the world
being all <u>down</u> <u>there</u>.

More Lovely Than Ever

From uncertainty about
what to do with divine gifts
to this new assuredness
that all is well within
and getting better all around:
lovelier than ever.

From the beauty of the fledgling
to the majestic wingspread of the great seabirds:
lovely as if time awaited <u>your</u> arrival
to become full moments.

Time for beauty:
moments lovelier
for your presence among them!

Welcome home, friend,
aren't those divine gifts I see
blossoming from your lips and eyes,
more lovely than ever!

Time After Time You Get It Right

It's not always right
'cause you choose right:
sometimes the ball takes a lucky bounce,
sometimes the one you love loves you back,
and every once in a while,
things come right all by themselves.

Time after time,
you get it right.

You go for it
and get what you want, mostly…

And every little once in a while,
it comes right to you!

Time after time…
you get it right.

If you think you're right,
that's alright,
but if you think you're more right,
that's fucked up!

Destination Home

Each comes here
naked to begin,
dressed to survive
and thrive
then naked again
on the way out.

But that's just half the story.

Some who come naked <u>stay that way</u>.
They dress their bodies, sure,
but their minds and bodies
are without cover,
without protection,
naked to each and every experience,
not just out, but up and out.

It's a tough life,
with more suffering,
but nothing they can't handle
and when they leave,
they are fully dressed
for the next available flight –
destination <u>HOME</u>!

For living in the open,
not weighed down,
they take flight
at departure:
destination <u>HOME</u>!

I want, I want

I know I can't be free —
but I want to be.

I can't be like cool
in all things —
but I want to!

I know I'll never
have wings and soar
like the great seabirds —
but I want to!

I see that my touch
is not yet quite heavenly —
but I want it to be!

You don't get here
to this high, windy place
above all and seeing all —
you don't get here
without giving all —
I don't give all
but <u>I want to</u>!

Aphorisms

Anything that doesn't kill you
is a wake-up call.

The tighter the web of troubles,
the better the chance to break free.

If you've got love playing downtown,
then the uptown lights grow brighter.

When a woman accepts the reality
of her own beauty and self-worth—
then all the belittling chatter of dickheads
is just white noise.

I love your fighting style

You've done all right for yourself
    and I love your fighting style!

You could have lost your dreams in life unkind,
you could have quit but you didn't,
you steered clear of kill-culture
    and I love your fighting style!

You fought off wilderness and the beast within,
you fought the darkness to a dawn
    and I love your fighting style!

You go rock this world, you bring your skills
to the gathering of the tribes
    we need your fighting style!
    we need your fighting style!

Live free, and love fearlessly
    and I love your fighting style!

3 Score and Ten

Wings rise
as the walls close in.

Mind can make a
heaven of hell
and I'm <u>on</u> to it!

From here the view is
never the same:
both in and out of the game
and I'm <u>in</u>to it.

The myth I think I'm living
and the myth I'm living:
both are worth the candle
and I'm <u>up</u> to it.

Shape-shifting vision quester
putting on and taking off cultural cloaks,
I'm up to it and I'm up for it:
wings rise as the walls close in.

Carry That Weight

Come on,
take it on.
You've got big shoulders,
carry that weight:
even burdens are not that great
when you've got big shoulders.

When you've got big shoulders,
nothing is all that heavy.

Come on,
take it on.

Eyes on the Prize, Freedom

Tell power what it needs to hear:
Yes, sir. Right away. You're right about that.
Eyes on the prize, freedom.

To make your way through the phonies,
hold on to your cojones.

The truth is for people who suffer as you do,
who hunger for a taste of greatness,
who dare to live for the impossible – as you do.

Eyes on the prize, freedom.

There's Something I Can Do

The world is falling apart
but there's something
I can do about it!

I can get a grip
on the problem:
<u>INEQUALITY</u>,
and get a handle
on the solution:
<u>RADICAL EQUALITY</u>,
every man and woman
a star.

I can be the change I seek:
that's something Gandhi said
that I can do.

I can change the world
by systematic practice of love:
that's something Rumi said
that I can do.

I can join others to protect
world and family,
work to achieve full human
and civil rights:
something Rachel Carson said
that I can do.

I can create,
and every action
changes outcomes,
that's something I can <u>do</u>!

The world is falling apart
and there's something
I can do about it!

Time Flowers

You've noticed the one-
liners in my stuff:

Wage slaves, What The Fuck!
Even hell is uptown.
Celebration is the revolution.
They hate you for being free.
A dangerous asshole will hurt you
in your point of view.
You're as generous a woman
as you can afford to be,
and as tough a bitch as you have to be.
DAMN! I'M GOOD!
When you do what you love, it's not work
your way is the highway.
You don't know
what you've got
til you got it goin' on.
All women fight back
because all women are under attack.
Managers get more money for the stress,
but they're just broke at a higher level.
In your own sweet time do what you do best.
You're too good for me,
I'm too good for you,
and that's good enough for us.
Truth without kindness is a lie.
The purpose of life is to have as much fun as possible.
I can smell blood in the water before the shark bites.
Build firewalls,
keep the killers out,
and keep your people free.
A young Bob Marley is rising up
in Jah-inspired splendor.
Love is Trail Mix in the night that lasts 'til dawn.
Nobody knows more than you,
no one knows less either.
Every man and every woman is a star
and we all shine on.

Without you, there's too many of them
and with you, we stand a chance.

These are time flowers,
set to go off at a later
time – and blossom!

Your Storm

with an eye to draw creations in,
with advance, winds so gentle petals scarcely murmur,
your storm reaches Caribbean shores.

your storm, named for boys who wouldn't,
for girls who would, be fiercely gentle, intensely still.

your storm, breaking loose, bounding up hills
and rooftops, brushing away what might not stand,
your storm with an eye to draw creations in!

your storm, swift to strike
swifter to bound away, never long to linger,
rapidly shifting moments within an abiding pattern,
blow winds and crack thunder!
lightning in the mind's eye of your storm!
your storm, no other. . .

creations riding your quicksilver beast to landfall,
then rain, rain, rain, drip, and sunshine clear.
after your storm, with an eye to draw creations in,
your storm.

My Time has Come and it's Apocalypse!

No better time! Wild days! Wild nights!

Dreams are on their way!
Wild days, wild nights,
and it's Apocalypse!

End of days, new day dawning!
And it's Apocalypse!

Been down so long, even hell is uptown!

End of days, new day dawning!
And it's Apocalypse!

The Lesbian Challenge

We do it better.
From the clitoris to the boardroom
we've got the right finger on the button.
We do it better.
The Lesbian challenge.

Long Story Short

She wanted what he couldn't give.
He needed what she wouldn't give.
Long story short:
They're still just friends, still lookin'.

Go Home to Mama

When you hook up, never expect someone
to carry your weight – or have to carry theirs.

If you can't deal with this,
go home to Mama.

When you've got it figured better,
return to the dating game.

Of course, dating does not involve your mama;
It's about being equal in all ways,
on a level field.

If you want more than your fair share,
go home to Mama!

Drop Me Like a Cat

Don't let me down easy,
like a dog I'll come back for more.

Like a dog, I'll figure you made it easy
because your heart wasn't in it.

Drop me like a cat,
just hold me out and let me fall.

Cat-like I'll land on my feet,
a little ruffled and likely to wander off,
vaguely seeking something else.

And I won't come back –
and that's good for both of us.

Don't let me down easy, just drop me –
drop me like a cat.

Shut This Shit Down

You go right on being hard on yourself – as long as you want to
Go ahead, be your own toughest critic – as long as you need to.

After all, you know your own lies and hypocrisies better than anyone,
why should you let yourself get away with it?

But when you've had enough of doing to yourself
what Mom and Dad did to you,
then shut this shit down.

When you're disgusted with the garbage they left for you to collect,
throw it away. Shut this shit down.

Shut this shit down. Shut this shit down.
No more self-putdowns, negativity be damned.
Give it up for a season, you're beautiful.

Forgive yourself now for what you couldn't do then
by acts of loving-kindness here and now.

Take a walk on the wild side,
see with pretty eyes.

Live free and love fearlessly:
It's the only light we've got in all this darkness.
Go on, shut this shit down.

www.ingramcontent.com/pod-product-compliance
Lightning Source LLC
Chambersburg PA
CBHW061300040426
42444CB00010B/2435